The Rosary

The Rosary

A Journey to the Beloved

by Gary Jansen

MADISON
PARK
PRESS™

NEW YORK

Published by Madison Park Press, 15 East 26th Street, New York, New York 10010.

Designed by Christos Peterson

ISBN: 1-58288-205-3

Printed in China

For the Beloved

Contents

⨕

Introduction

The Rosary is a popular and often misunderstood prayer that the faithful, the broken, the curious, and the weary have turned to for almost a thousand years. Though traditionally considered a Catholic act of devotion, the Rosary, with its primary focus on the life, death, and resurrection of Christ Jesus, is ultimately a *catholic*, or universal, prayer that can appeal to Christians of all faiths and denominations. It's a prayer of transformation, a prayer of peace, a prayer of hope. It is also a prayer that changed my life.

Some years back I was suffering through a dark—and seemingly endless—night of the soul. This wasn't depression. I had suffered through depressions before; this was something different. This was something frightening. Though I'd always had what I considered a confrontational relationship with God—more often than not, *my will* was not *His will*—I always felt His presence in my life. But, not this time. This time I felt nothing, like that initial moment when you wake from a dreamless sleep. For the first time in my life I doubted the existence of God.

One day I was sitting in traffic when I looked over to my right to see a bumper sticker on a minivan. It read: *Knock and the door will be opened*. "Yeah, right," I mumbled under my breath. I must have been daydreaming because the car behind me honked its horn and when I looked up, traffic had moved ahead. As I pulled away I noticed for the first time in a long while the set of rosary beads that hung from my rearview mirror. I had gotten so used to them that I stopped discerning that they were in front of my face every day.

I don't know why I did what I did next, but I took those beads down and started praying in the car. Now, I had prayed the Rosary many times over the years—and quickly abandoned it just as many times—but a new hope stirred inside me. Maybe it was the bumper sticker, maybe it was a last-ditch effort to get through to God and assuage this gloomy fear that was following me everywhere I went, but I decided right then and there that I would work through the boredom and frustration I experienced in the past and pray the Rosary every day until God opened a door for me. If knocking hadn't worked, maybe the rattling of beads would.

So I prayed and within a couple weeks the combination of prayer and meditation that is essential to the Rosary made me feel less tense, but I still wasn't experiencing God's presence. Nonetheless, I was committed and I stayed the course. Knock. Knock. Knock.

Around this same time in my life, I had started working out at a local gym. One evening, a trainer I had never seen before walked over to me after I had finished a set of exercises and said, "You're carrying too much weight."

"Excuse me?" I answered back.

"Too much weight," he repeated. "You're doing the exercise wrong. You're going to hurt yourself."

I just stared at him. If someone had snapped a picture of me, I'm sure the look on my face would have been that stupid, crooked, toothy half-smile I have when I feel like I'm being insulted.

The trainer pulled the pin out of the machine and reduced the weight by more than half and proceeded to show me the proper form for the exercise.

"You try it," he said.

I did. And I could barely lift the lighter weight.

As I walked home later that evening, the trainer's words kept moving inside my head—for no other reason at the time than that they reminded me of the Beatles song "Carry That Weight." Later that night, as I began praying the Rosary (which had become my before-sleep ritual) and meditating on the Sorrowful Mysteries of Christ, it hit me.

You're carrying too much weight.

It was then that words from the Bible I hadn't thought of in years flooded my ears, "Come to me, all you who are weary and burdened, and I will give you rest" (Matt. 11:28).

God had not abandoned me, I just hadn't been listening. It was that night that I realized that the Rosary wasn't a way of getting God's attention, but was a way of getting *me to pay attention*. My life was never the same again.

꒰ꜟ꒱

The Rosary can change your life by opening your eyes and ears to God's voice. This book is not intended to be an exhaustive study on this sacred prayer. Rather, it's a short introduction on how to listen for God's words in your day-to-day life and a reminder that you are never alone. At its core, this is a little book about prayer, one of the greatest gifts that God has ever given us. It is also an invitation to fall in love with the Beloved. And if you are already head-over-heels here is an opportunity to keep tumbling.

What Is the Rosary?

≋

I magine for a moment that you have just fallen in love with the person of your dreams. Picture it right now. Picture your ideal. Picture your beloved. This person is beautiful, smart, and wise. This person is caring and loves children. This person values friendship in a way you've never experienced, and when you are in the presence of your beloved you feel whole: energized, perplexed, inspired, and amazed.

Now, you've experienced loves in the past, but this relationship is different. It's mutual and nurturing. The more deeply you fall for your beloved, the more human you feel. Could it be that your soul was asleep for years and that this person has awakened you, has even resurrected your spirit, your will, your desire? You feel changed, because you *are* changed. You feel that maybe the world around you had been covered in thin diaphanous veils and with each step you take toward your beloved, a layer is removed. Your vision becomes clearer and clearer. Colors are more colorful, sounds are crisper, you hear music in noise. For the first time since you were a child you experience wonder.

So continue imagining your beloved and continue seeing your relationship expanding, growing with each word, with each action, with each hope. Time passes; it has just been the two of you for some time. Then your beloved asks you to meet the parents.

What is your reaction now? Are you anxious? Nervous? *What are they going to think of me? Am I good enough? Are they going to see through to my faults?* It's one thing to be in a relationship, you think; it's an entirely different thing to add the parents. You've done a pretty good job of hiding some of these things from your beloved, but parents always know, *especially* mothers.

Your beloved senses your anxiety and reassures you that everything will be fine. The fateful day arrives and you walk to the parents' home. As your beloved takes your hand, you notice that your palms are sweaty.

Your beloved knocks. The door opens. You meet Mom.

And she turns out to be the nicest person you've ever met.

She welcomes you into the family and she radiates kindness and beauty. All that worrying, all those moments of self-doubt subside, and in a matter of seconds you feel excited to be in her presence. You look around and don't see the father, but you sense that he is everywhere in this home.

Now let's take a step back. You have never experienced a love like the one you have with your beloved, and, while you feel an openness, you admit to yourself that this person can be a mystery to you. You have questions. It's not that you don't feel close to your beloved, it's just that you begin to hunger and thirst to know everything about this love that has come into your life. And to be perfectly honest, you feel intimidated, because your beloved is such a complete person, and you feel, more often than not, less than whole.

What were you like as a child? What were your parents doing before they had you? What were your friends like? Did you ever get lost? What were some of the loneliest times of your life? Why did you come into my life?

You've held off asking some of these questions of your beloved but here in front of Mom, you feel strangely comfortable to let loose. It's as if she is standing there ready to embrace you and help you understand everything. Who better than your beloved's mother to answer all these questions swirling in your mind? Who better to provide insight than the woman who carried your beloved in her body for nine months and who experienced the pain and joy of bringing her child into the world?

You begin to ask all your questions and this woman who you've just met seemingly transforms into your own mother. She smiles and takes down a scrapbook and the two of you begin looking at pictures. *This is a picture of me when I first found out I was going to have a baby,* she says. *This is a picture of my cousin and me, we were both pregnant at the same time. Here's one right after the birth. So many people came to visit us. Here are a few pictures of a wedding we attended and this is a picture of . . .*

So you sit in her presence and page through the scrapbook of their lives. These pictures tell stories and you begin to understand what was once a mystery. You feel this family's happiness, their sorrows, their illuminations, and the glory of their lives. All of a sudden, the worries, the fears, the doubts, the brokenness, the distractions that you seem to feel on a daily basis fall away and you are transformed by love.

That is the Rosary.

ॐ

Wait, you may be saying, what does all this have to do with the Rosary? Isn't the Rosary some long complicated prayer where you say the Hail Mary a couple of hundred times while holding a set of beads?

Yes, but not exactly. The Rosary is a prayer and it is longer than most in the Christian tradition but it's a simple prayer and, like all simple things, it is beautifully complex once you get to know it.

Yet, the Rosary is more than just a *prayer*; it is a journey to the beloved, an invitation to fall in love with Christ by sitting in the presence of His mother and observing through the prism of her life and *your* life the radiance of divine revelation. Anyone can say a prayer or go to Church or quote the Bible, but it is only through loving Christ and entering into a relationship that we can, through patience, meditation, and contemplation, align our earthly desires and longings with the will of God.

ॐ

According to *Merriam-Webster's Collegiate Dictionary*, the word rosary is derived from the Latin word *rosarium,* meaning rose garden, and has been a form of prayer—traditionally said with the aid of beads, since before the time of the

Reformation. One characteristic that makes this prayer different from many others is the use of repetition. Popularized by the Order of St. Dominic in the fifteenth century, the Rosary is a cycle of repeating prayers that combines meditation with devotion. It is comprised of four sets of mysteries—or time periods—from the Gospels and are named the joyful, the sorrowful, the luminous, and the glorious. Each set of mysteries in turn is made up of five specific events from the life of Christ. A decade, which is just a fancy word for a prayer repeated ten times, traditionally the Hail Mary, is said for each event. There are prayers that begin the Rosary, prayers between each decade, and prayers that end the Rosary. While the focus on the Rosary is always Jesus Christ, the guide connecting the mysteries is Mary herself who takes us by the hand and leads us through the miraculous journey of her Son's life.

While you can pray all four sets of mysteries in one sitting, it is more common for people to choose one set and focus attention on those events. The Rosary can be a difficult prayer in the beginning. Many will balk at the idea of repeating the same prayers over and over again (how boring!), but through practice and through imaginative meditation you'll come to realize, as Romano Guardini notes in *The Rosary of Our Lady*, that the greatest things in life are repetitious: the cycles of life, the turning of seasons, the beating of a heart, breathing. Life *is* repetition.

One misconception about the Rosary that makes many non-Catholics suspicious is that it's a prayer to Mary. This isn't true. One does not pray *to* Mary when he or she says the

Rosary, a person prays *with* Mary, the way someone would pray with another person at church or in a prayer group.

Imagine this. Suppose I ran into you on the street. You're a prayerful person and you know I am too. You are going through hard times. Maybe your parents are ill. Maybe you have lost your job. Maybe you are dealing with the death of a loved one. We talk for a few minutes and as we part you ask me to pray for you. I assure you I will.

Praying the Rosary is no different than that exchange. It is spiritual union, an act of love for the benefit of another. As Pope John Paul II stated in his 2002 apostolic letter, *On the Most Holy Rosary*, the Rosary is a prayer of learning and illumination that allows, "The principal events of the life of Jesus Christ [to] pass before the eyes of the soul . . . they put us in living communion with Jesus through—we might say—the heart of his Mother."

Ultimately, the Rosary is *your* prayer and can be prayed the way you see fit. It's a gift from God and there is much to be learned from such a generous offering. But if the Hail Mary is the one thing that is preventing you from taking part in this divinely inspired exercise, then say the Our Father instead. And if the Hail, Holy Queen, which ends the Rosary cycle, is also not to your liking, then recite the Jesus Prayer, "Lord Jesus Christ, Son of the Living God, have mercy on me."

The Mysteries of the Rosary

A mystery is something that leaves you feeling puzzled and perplexed. We see this commonly in suspense movies and novels. Usually, the main character is presented with a bewildering situation—something has happened but why and who is responsible? For the rest of the story, the hero or heroine tries to uncover the answers to those questions. The best mysteries are the ones with twists and turns—stories that keep you scratching your head and push you to your intellectual limits.

The stories that make up the Rosary are the greatest mysteries of all time. They are filled with colorful characters and events, there are twists and turns, and they are fundamentally a call for investigation. But unlike an ordinary detective novel, the Rosary asks that you check your intellect at the door. These are scenes of faith and, while it's important to ask all the questions a seasoned private investigator would: *Why did this happen, how did this happen, who's responsible, how do I understand what's going on*, this prayer asks for something different. These are meditative investigations, ones that are best approached by *not* thinking. How is that possible, you ask? By moving from the realm of the mind to the realm of the heart—by *experiencing* the mysteries.

But what does that mean? Imagine that a friend of yours has just heard some bad news. He or she is justifiably emotional and upset. Now, you could talk to your friend about what happened or you could just sit quietly and be in his presence and empathize with him. In the latter scenario, your actions speak louder than your words ever could. You are aware of everything around you, but you're not talking, you're not thinking, you are just *there* and in the presence of a friend. You are experiencing the moment.

Or imagine that you are on the pediatric floor of a hospital and you are standing in the company of a couple who has just had a baby. Surely words of joy will be exchanged among everyone present, but at a certain point everyone stops talking and looks at this new life that has come into the world. The mystery of life. Words can't be attached to it because the event is ineffable, but you are experiencing something. That experience is a movement from the mind to the heart.

꒰

The Rosary was originally comprised of three sets of mysteries: the joyful, the sorrowful, and the glorious, which corresponded to different time periods in the life of Jesus Christ and His mother, Mary. These groups of mysteries dealt with the early years of Christ's life, His Passion, and His

Resurrection. In his 2002 apostolic letter, *On the Most Holy Rosary,* Pope John Paul II added a fourth set of mysteries, the luminous or mysteries of light, which centered on the redemptive power of Christ's ministry.

What follows are the four sets of mysteries and the five events contained within each.

Joyful

The Annunciation
The Visitation
The Nativity
The Presentation of the Infant Jesus in the Temple
The Finding of Jesus in the Temple

Luminous

The Baptism in the River Jordan
The Wedding at Cana
The Proclamation of the Kingdom of God
The Transfiguration of Jesus
The Last Supper

Sorrowful

The Agony in the Garden
The Scourging at the Pillar
The Crowning with Thorns
The Carrying of the Cross
The Crucifixion

Glorious

The Resurrection
The Ascension
The Descent of the Holy Spirit
The Assumption of Mary*
The Crowning of Mary*

The joyful mysteries center on the miracle of "the incar-nation" (*On the Most Holy Rosary*, page 27), where the divine and the human were made known in the body and soul of Jesus Christ. The Annunciation begins the mysteries as the angel Gabriel descends upon the young virgin named Mary and tells her that she is going to be the mother of the Messiah. The scene then shifts to the Visitation where Mary journeys to visit her much older cousin, Elizabeth, who is also with child. Elizabeth will give birth to a son, John, who will become the Baptist who will prepare the way for Jesus' ministry. The Nativity follows, that joyous occasion when Mary gives birth to Jesus and lays Him in the manger and where shepherds and wise men journey to bow before the King of all creation. Eight days later, Jesus is presented at the temple, as is customary in Jewish tradition, and the Holy

*Author's note: In his book, *The Rosary of Our Lady* (Sophia Institute Press, New Hampshire, 1983), Romano Guardini, a twentieth-century Italian-born Catholic priest and theologian, talks briefly about substituting the last two glo-rious mysteries with two events that "look for a clearer projection of a truth that governs our present life: namely, the waiting for Christ's return." For Protestants, who are uncomfortable focusing on the Catholic ideas of the Assumption and the Crowning of Mary, two alternate mysteries may be used: The Second Coming, which centers on Christ's return; and The Kingdom of God, which "is already ours, even if only as a promise and a beginning."

Family meets a man named Simeon, a man filled with the Holy Spirit. The joyful mysteries then conclude with the story of Mary and Joseph finding the lost Jesus in the temple, preaching to the scholars and holy people.

The journey to the Beloved continues with the luminous mysteries and begins with the baptism of Jesus in the river Jordan. As His cousin John pours the water over Jesus' body the light of God shines down on His Beloved and appears to all present. We then move on to the story of the Wedding at Cana. A feast and celebration is already underway when the wine runs out. Mary spurs Jesus to help and the reluctant hero performs His first public miracle. Afterward the scene changes to Christ proclaiming that the Kingdom of God is at hand. It's not tomorrow or yesterday, it's in the here and now. We are then brought to the story of the Transfiguration where the light of God's love shines through His Son, and Christ takes his place between Moses and the prophet Elijah. This set of mysteries ends with the story of the Last Supper as Jesus shares His final meal with His friends and disciples and offers them His body and blood, the bread and wine of life.

We then move to the sorrowful mysteries, which center on the Passion of Christ. The Agony in the Garden is a painful time for Jesus who asks, "Father, if you are willing, take this cup from me; yet not my will, but yours be done" (Luke 22:42). The story continues with the Scourging at the Pillar where Christ is brutally beaten and flogged by the Roman authorities. He is mocked even more as His tormentors fashion a mock crown, made of nail-like thorns, and place it on His head. Jesus is then forced to carry His cross through the sun-dried streets of Jerusalem. This set of mysteries concludes with the Crucifixion. Christ is nailed to the Cross and almost everyone has abandoned Him except for his beloved mother and His friends John and Mary Magdalene.

The final set of mysteries is the glorious and leads with the Resurrection. Jesus has risen from the dead and with Him rise our hopes for eternal salvation. We move on to the miracle of the Ascension, where Christ blesses His friends and is taken up to Heaven. The mysteries continue with Mary and the Apostles receiving the gift of the Holy Spirit and setting out to preach the Good News of the Resurrection. The set concludes with God the Father blessing Mary by assuming her body into Heaven and crowning her in glory.

Prayer

⧉

God is a chatterbox. I say that only slightly tongue-in-cheek, because God never stops talking to us. The reason we suffer, the reason we feel fear, the reason we feel disjointed and unfocused and lost is because we don't realize that at any given moment the answer to all our questions, the balm for all our suffering is right in front of us. We just don't realize it. We're not *aware*. We don't hear God speaking to us. Why? Because most of the time we don't shut up.

Have you ever tried to listen to two conversations at one time? It's nearly impossible—you get fragments of one and fragments of another and neither makes sense. Have you ever tried to listen to two conversations when *you* are one of the people speaking? You can't understand what the other person is saying!

Now, you might be objecting, I'm a quiet person, I'm respectful, I don't talk a lot and I'm a good listener, so why can't I still hear God. It's because for many of us even if we are not vocalizing, we are thinking. We don't let our minds and souls rest. Instead, they race with ideas and questions and worries.

Try this short experiment:

Find a watch or some kind of clock that has a second

hand on it. Take a few moments to relax. Take a few deep breaths. Now, try *not* to think about anything for ten seconds.

Go.

Did you think of something? Maybe it was a traffic ticket you forgot to pay or a phone call you have to make or maybe you started thinking about what you should eat for dinner or what kind of clothes you need to buy your child for school. It's almost impossible to stop thinking. Thinking is a habit. And for some of us it is a very bad habit.

So if we are constantly thinking or constantly speaking or constantly doing something or constantly drowning out God with our own personal white noise, what can we do to center ourselves to allow the voice of God to enter into us? How can we start listening?

Prayer.

But isn't prayer about *talking* to God? No one ever taught us how to listen during prayer.

Almost everyone believes that prayer is communicating with God. This is true, but keep in mind that prayer is essentially a *tool* for communication, for getting your mind, body, and soul to a state where you can communicate with God. It's a way of quieting your restless heart, your restless mind, your restless soul—it is a tool to help you focus.

One of the best ways to bring you to that state is through repetitious prayer like the Rosary. The combination of repeating prayers and meditation automatically calms our minds. There's no room for our worries or our problems. Let God take care of them. God will dress us and feed us and protect us. We just need to stop thinking and start listening.

Why Do We Pray the Rosary?

The Rosary isn't the only prayer to help you to hear God, but for me it's been the most effective. Most of us go through life not *living in the moment*. This phrase has become a cliché in self-help circles. Books and motivational gurus tell us that if we only lived in the moment we would all be happier and more fulfilled. I actually buy this cliché. When we are not living in the moment, we are missing out on the gift of experience. I know personally, I am often never where I am. I'm somewhere else. I am either thinking about the future or worrying about the past. I am either planning to do something or regretting that I haven't done something. I am almost never *here and now*. But the Rosary has helped me move closer to the present, closer to the Kingdom of God, which is at hand *right now*. The Rosary refocuses my attention away from my worries and toward the face of Christ.

Now, the Rosary is undoubtedly a *spiritual* exercise, but a part of its power comes from the fact that it is also a *physical* exercise. Because of the structure, because of the repetition and the focus on meditation—which is nothing more than observing a scene and not attaching words to it—the Rosary has a soothing effect on the body. It helps to regulate breathing, it reduces stress, and it relaxes muscles. It's soothing. A friend of mine once berated himself for saying the Rosary and falling asleep. Why should he be upset? He should be thankful. To fall asleep in the arms of God, one could not be more blessed!

The more you practice the prayer and the more you explore the mysteries and how they relate to your life, the more your day-to-day worries will be eclipsed by the life of Christ. When you are in this state, even though you are doing many things at once, fingering a bead, saying a prayer, contemplating a mystery, your eyes and ears open to God. You begin to wake. And there are times when there will just be silence. That's okay, because the Rosary follows you through your day-to-day life. You'll be more aware of the people and things around you. You'll have more appreciation for creation. You'll feel more alive.

But wait, you say, I'm reciting prayers during the Rosary, how is that being quiet? Yes, you will be saying prayers and vocalizing either internally or externally, but what those prayers are doing is replacing the other thoughts that are inside your mind. Over time, the more you pray the more automatic the individual prayers will become. That's okay, because what we want to achieve is a refocusing toward God. The words, while important, are secondary to the meditative experience. God knows our words even before we articulate them, even before they are born in our minds and heart. By turning our gaze to Christ we begin to understand what it is we truly need in life. God already knows. We, on the other hand, have to learn.

Many people get frustrated with prayer and stop because they don't feel that God is listening, but we can never be out of community with God. We may feel like we are, but feelings don't equate to truth. You know your feelings can change in an instant. You may feel happy one day, sad the next. You may feel confident one day and unsure the next. What has changed? Are you not the same person? If God were to strip you of your doubts and your assurances who would you be?

Imagine for a moment that you want to talk to a friend; so you call him on the telephone, but he isn't home. You leave a message. A few days go by and your friend hasn't returned your call. So you call again and leave another message. Days pass and still no return call. You feel angry. Why is this friend ignoring you? How rude! A few more days pass and when you least expect it you receive a phone call. It is your friend graciously apologizing for not calling you back sooner, but reminding you that he was out of town and how he asked you to water his plants. All of a sudden your anger subsides. You felt abandoned, but you weren't. You didn't pay attention to what your friend told you!

Getting the Most out of the Rosary

Using Your Imagination

One of the ways of getting more out of the Rosary is to use your imagination. After you've begun meditating on a mystery, start imagining yourself in the scene. For instance, if you are contemplating the Annunciation you may try to envision the scene when Gabriel appeared to Mary. Is it in the morning or evening? Is the air cool or stagnant? Is the room decorated in any way? What is Mary wearing? Imagine what the angel may have looked like to her. Was Gabriel a ray of light or an image of a man? What is the reaction on Mary's face when she receives the news? What happens after the angel leaves? Continue the story, not necessarily with words but with images, become fully present in the mystery, and then reflect on how the scene relates to your own life. What can you learn about Mary's desire to accept the Will of God?

Or place yourself at the Wedding at Cana. Maybe you are a hopeless eavesdropper and you overhear the exchange between Jesus and His mother. Look around at the people having a good time. Look at the servants. Think of the excitement. Is there music at the feast? What kind of music is in the background? Are people laughing? Are people dancing? If wine is such an integral part of the celebration what would happen if the hosts ran out? How would the atmosphere change? What is the look on Christ's face when He performs His first public miracle? What are the reactions of the disciples? What does the wine taste like? Then contemplate the miracles in your own life. Are there times when you can metaphorically change water into wine?

Or imagine the Passion. Imagine the brutality of the beatings. Imagine what Jesus might have looked like as the whips tore at His flesh or the pain of standing up after being beaten. Would you be able to endure this for God? Imagine what must have been going on inside of Christ's mind at the time. What is He thinking as He stands before the Romans? What is Christ feeling? What are the reactions of the Romans or the common people who are witnessing these events? Imagine yourself being witness to the Passion. How would you feel if you watched someone being treated like this? How would you feel if it was a friend of yours? How would you feel if it was an enemy? Then come back and contemplate the meaning of suffering in your life. What can you learn about bearing responsibility in your own life?

Or imagine that you are tending the area near Christ's tomb and the women come by early one morning to anoint the body. You watch them and watch the Roman guard roll away the stone. Then you hear the shouts of joy and the cries of faith and overhear the exuberance of the women. He is risen! What is your reaction? What do the women look like? What is the reaction of the guards? Can you see inside the tomb? What do you see there? What is the morning like? Are there birds in the trees? Is the path made of stone or of dirt? Then bring your meditation back to Christ and focus and pray for a deeper understanding of the glory of the Resurrection. What does Christ's rising mean in your life?

By using your imagination, you make the mysteries personal to you. On a physical level, the more you can experience something, the more you feel moved by it. Christ, even in all His divinity, experienced the world in human ways— He felt pain and hope and disappointment and love and friendship the way we do. So, while keeping our eyes focused on the Good News of Christ we can expand the stories personally through the realm of our imagination. The way I imagine Christ's smile may be different from the way you imagine His smile, but that doesn't matter. What matters is entering into the scene, becoming part of God's word, and attempting in our human way to experience what He experienced.

Breathing

In the beginning, the Rosary can be a little like driving a car for the first time. There is a lot to remember. You have to remember the mystery, you need to remember the order of the prayers, then say your prayers and while saying your prayers contemplate the mystery. This can be a struggle and you'll find your mind wandering, but over time you'll be distracted less and be drawn closer into the beauty of this Rose of Christ.

I would like to suggest adding another element to your prayer. Breathing. Many of us aren't conscious of our own breathing, but regulating our breath during meditation and prayer will lead to a greater alignment of our mind, body, and soul. The following is a simple breathing pattern incorporating the Hail Mary. This exercise, however, can be used for any prayer whether it's the Our Father or the Jesus Prayer or whichever you choose. It is by no means necessary for saying the Rosary, but it's an added element that yields great rewards mentally, physically, and spiritually. And if you find the exercise below too difficult or if it's uncomfortable to perform, feel free to find your own rhythm and create your own pattern.

Try this:

Breathe in through your nose and say to yourself
Hail Mary, full of grace, the lord is with thee

Breathe out your mouth, saying to yourself
Blessed art thou among women and blessed is the fruit of thy womb, Jesus

Breathe in through your nose, saying to yourself
Holy Mary, Mother of God,

Breathe out your mouth, finishing your prayer
Pray for us sinners, now and at the hour of our death, amen.

How to Pray the Rosary

With Beads

1. Choose a set of Mysteries, make the Sign of the Cross, and recite the Apostles' Creed* while holding the crucifix.

2. On the first bead say an Our Father or the Lord's Prayer.

3. On the three beads that follow, recite the Hail Mary* for each bead and meditate on three virtues: Faith, Hope, and Charity.

4. Recite the Glory Be between your last bead and the next.

5. On the following bead, say an Our Father and begin meditating on the first mystery.

6. Moving to your right, begin praying the Hail Mary. Repeat this prayer for each bead.

*For Protestants, please note that the Lord's Prayer or the Jesus Prayer can be used as a substitution for the Hail Mary and the Hail, Holy Queen. Protestants may also substitute the Nicene Creed for the Apostles' Creed.

7. After reciting a Hail Mary on each of the ten beads recite the Glory Be. This completes one decade.

8. Repeat steps 5-7 for each mystery and conclude your prayer with a Hail, Holy Queen. Finish with the Sign of the Cross.

Without Beads

While anyone can pray the Rosary by using his or her fingers to keep track of the number of prayers recited, the second part of this book is designed to lead you through your spiritual journey in an undistracted manner—with or without the use of rosary beads. The prayers that begin the Rosary can be found at the start of the next section. The mysteries then follow with passages selected from scripture that correspond to the chosen event. Each reading is accompanied by a painting that is offered here to help you visually meditate on the mysteries. Along the edges of the left-hand pages are eleven markers that you can use to keep track of your prayers by running your thumb along the side. For every event, begin with an Our Father on the first marker. On the next ten markers recite the Hail Mary, finish with a Glory Be, and then proceed to the next mystery. The last part of the second section contains the prayers necessary to conclude the Rosary.

No Worries

God is all around us, but so many times we allow worry and fear to block God out of our lives. As you move onto the second section of this book, which includes a visual journey through the Rosary, I would like to leave you these words from Christ's Sermon on the Mount. These are words to keep in mind every minute of every day, while you are praying the Rosary or while you're just living your life.

Therefore I tell you, do not worry about your life, what you will eat or drink; or about your body, what you will wear. Is not life more important than food, and the body more important than clothes? Look at the birds of the air; they do not sow or reap or store away in barns, and yet your heavenly Father feeds them. Are you not much more valuable than they? Who of you by worrying can add a single hour to his life?

And why do you worry about clothes? See how the lilies of the field grow. They do not labor or spin. Yet I tell you that not even Solomon in all his splendor was dressed like one of these. . . . Therefore do not worry about tomorrow, for tomorrow will worry about itself. Each day has enough trouble of its own.

Matt. 6:25-30, 34

The Rosary

The Sign of the Cross

In the name of the Father, and of the Son, and of the Holy Spirit. Amen.

≈

The Apostles' Creed

I believe in God, the Father almighty, creator of heaven and earth. I believe in Jesus Christ, his only Son, our Lord. He was conceived by the power of the Holy Spirit and born of the Virgin Mary. He suffered under Pontius Pilate, was crucified, died and was buried. He descended to the dead. On the third day he rose again. He ascended into heaven, and is seated at the right hand of the Father. He will come again to judge the living and the dead. I believe in the Holy Spirit, the holy Catholic Church, the communion of saints, the forgiveness of sins, the resurrection of the body and the life everlasting. Amen.

Our Father

Our Father, who art in heaven, hallowed be Thy name; Thy Kingdom come; Thy Will be done, on earth as it is in heaven. Give us this day our daily bread; and forgive us our trespasses as we forgive those who trespass against us. And lead us not into temptation but deliver us from evil. Amen.

Hail Mary

Hail Mary, full of grace, the Lord is with thee; blessed are thou among women and blessed is the fruit of thy womb, Jesus. Holy Mary, Mother of God, pray for us sinners, now and at the hour of our death. Amen. (Repeat three times.)

Glory Be

Glory Be to the Father, and to the Son, and to the Holy Spirit; as it was in the beginning, is now and ever shall be, world without end. Amen.

The Joyful Mysteries

The First Joyful Mystery

The Annunciation

God sent the angel Gabriel to Nazareth, a town in Galilee, to a virgin pledged to be married to a man named Joseph, a descendant of David. The virgin's name was Mary. The angel went to her and said, "Greetings, you who are highly favored! The Lord is with you. . . ."

"Do not be afraid, Mary, you have found favor with God. You will be with child and give birth to a son, and you are to give him the name Jesus. . . ."

"The Holy Spirit will come upon you, and the power of the Most High will overshadow you. So the holy one to be born will be called the Son of God. . . ."

"I am the Lord's servant," Mary answered. "May it be to me as you have said."

Luke 1:26-28, 30-31, 35, 38

The Second Joyful Mystery

The Visitation

At that time Mary got ready and hurried to a town in the hill country of Judea, where she entered Zechariah's home and greeted Elizabeth. When Elizabeth heard Mary's greeting, the baby leaped in her womb and Elizabeth was filled with the Holy Spirit. In a loud voice she exclaimed: "Blessed are you among women and blessed is the child you will bear! . . . Blessed is she who has believed that what the Lord has said to her will be accomplished!"

Luke 1:39-42, 45

The Third Joyful Mystery

The Nativity

In those days Caesar Augustus issued a decree that a census should be taken of the entire Roman world. . . . And everyone went to his own town to register.

So Joseph also went up from the town of Nazareth in Galilee to Judea, to Bethlehem the town of David, because he belonged to the house and line of David. He went there to register with Mary, who was pledged to be married to him and was expecting a child. While they were there, the time came for the baby to be born, and she gave birth to her firstborn, a son. She wrapped him in cloths and placed him in a manger, because there was no room for them in the inn.

Luke 2:1, 3-7

The Fourth Joyful Mystery

The Presentation of the Infant Jesus in the Temple

On the eighth day, when it was time to circumcise him, he was named Jesus, the name the angel had given him before he had been conceived. . . .

Now there was a man in Jerusalem called Simeon, who was righteous and devout. He was waiting for the consolation of Israel, and the Holy Spirit was upon him. It had been revealed to him by the Holy Spirit that he would not die before he had seen the Lord's Christ. Moved by the Spirit, he went into the temple courts. When the parents brought in the child Jesus to do for him what the custom of the Law required, Simeon took him in his arms and praised God, saying:

"Sovereign Lord, as you have promised, you now dismiss your servant in peace. For my eyes have seen your salvation."

Luke 2:21, 25-30

The Fifth Joyful Mystery

The Finding of Jesus in the Temple

Every year his parents went to Jerusalem for the Feast of the Passover. When he was twelve years old, they went up to the Feast, according to the custom. After the Feast was over, while his parents were returning home, the boy Jesus stayed behind in Jerusalem, but they were unaware of it. Thinking he was in their company, they traveled on for a day. Then they began looking for him among their relatives and friends. When they did not find him, they went back to Jerusalem to look for him. After three days they found him in the temple courts, sitting among the teachers, listening to them and asking them questions. Everyone who heard him was amazed at his understanding and his answers. When his parents saw him, they were astonished. His mother said to him, "Son, why have you treated us like this? Your father and I have been anxiously searching for you."

"Why were you searching for me?" he asked. "Didn't you know I had to be in my Father's house?"

Luke 2:41-49

The Luminous Mysteries

The First Luminous Mystery
The Baptism in the River Jordan

Then Jesus came from Galilee to the Jordan to be baptized by John. . . . As soon as Jesus was baptized, he went up out of the water. At that moment heaven was opened, and he saw the Spirit of God descending like a dove and lighting on him. And a voice from heaven said, "This is my Son, whom I love; with him I am well pleased."

Matt. 3:13, 16-17

The Second Luminous Mystery

The Wedding at Cana

On the third day a wedding took place at Cana in Galilee. Jesus' mother was there, and Jesus and his disciples had also been invited to the wedding. When the wine was gone, Jesus' mother said to him, "They have no more wine."

"Dear woman, why do you involve me?" Jesus replied. "My time has not yet come."

His mother said to the servants, "Do whatever he tells you."

Nearby stood six stone water jars, the kind used by the Jews for ceremonial washing, each holding from twenty to thirty gallons.

Jesus said to the servants, "Fill the jars with water"; so they filled them to the brim.

Then he told them, "Now draw some out and take it to the master of the banquet."

They did so, and the master of the banquet tasted the water that had been turned into wine . . .

John 2:1-9

The Third Luminous Mystery

The Proclamation of the Kingdom of God

When Jesus heard that John had been put in prison, he returned to Galilee. Leaving Nazareth, he went and lived in Capernaum, which was by the lake in the area of Zebulun and Naphtali—to fulfill what was said through the prophet Isaiah:

> Land of Zebulun and land of Naphtali,
> the way to the sea, along the Jordan,
> Galilee of the Gentiles—
> the people living in darkness
> have seen a great light;
> on those living in the land of the shadow of death
> a light has dawned.

From that time on Jesus began to preach, "Repent, for the kingdom of heaven is near."

Matt. 4:12-17

The Fourth Luminous Mystery

The Transfiguration of Jesus

[Jesus] took Peter, John, and James with him and went up onto a mountain to pray. As he was praying, the appearance of his face changed, and his clothes became as bright as a flash of lightning. Two men, Moses and Elijah, appeared in glorious splendor, talking with Jesus. They spoke about his departure, which he was about to bring to fulfillment at Jerusalem. Peter and his companion were very sleepy, but when they became fully awake, they saw his glory and the two men standing with him . . . [A] cloud appeared and enveloped them, and they were afraid as they entered the cloud. A voice came from the cloud saying, "This is my Son, whom I have chosen; listen to him." When the voice had spoken they found that Jesus was alone. The disciples kept this to themselves, and told no one at that time what they had seen.

Luke 9:28-32, 34-36

The Fifth Luminous Mystery

The Last Supper

Then came the day of Unleavened Bread on which the Passover lamb had to be sacrificed. Jesus sent Peter and John, saying, "Go and make preparations for us to eat the Passover."

When the hour came, Jesus and his apostles reclined at the table. And he said to them, "I have eagerly desired to eat this Passover with you before I suffer. For I tell you, I will not eat it again until it finds fulfillment in the kingdom of God."

And he took bread, gave thanks and broke it, and gave it to them, saying, "This is my body given for you; do this in remembrance of me."

In the same way, after the supper he took the cup, saying, "This cup is the new covenant in my blood, which is poured out for you."

Luke 22:7, 14-16, 19-20

The Sorrowful Mysteries

The First Sorrowful Mystery

The Agony in the Garden

Then Jesus went with his disciples to a place called Gethsemane, and he said to them, "Sit here while I go over there and pray." He took Peter and the two sons of Zebedee along with him, and he began to be sorrowful and troubled. Then he said to them, "My soul is overwhelmed with sorrow to the point of death. Stay here and keep watch with me."

Going a little farther, he fell with his face to the ground and prayed, "My Father, if it is possible, may this cup be taken from me. Yet not as I will, but as you will."

Then he returned to his disciples and found them sleeping . . .

Matt. 26:36-40

The Second Sorrowful Mystery

The Scourging at the Pillar

"What shall I do, then, with the one you call the king of the Jews?" Pilate asked them.

"Crucify him!" they shouted.

"Why? What crime has he committed?" asked Pilate.

But they shouted all the louder, "Crucify him!"

Wanting to satisfy the crowd, Pilate released Barabbas to them. He had Jesus flogged, and handed him over to be crucified.

Mark 15:12-15

The Third Sorrowful Mystery

The Crowning with Thorns

The soldiers led Jesus away into the palace (that is, the Praetorium) and called together the whole company of soldiers. They put a purple robe on him, then twisted together a crown of thorns and set it on him. And they began to call out to him, "Hail, king of the Jews!" Again and again they struck him on the head with a staff and spit on him. Falling on their knees, they paid homage to him. And when they had mocked him, they took off the purple robe and put his own clothes on him. Then they led him out to crucify him.

Mark 15:16-20

The Fourth Sorrowful Mystery

The Carrying of the Cross

So the soldiers took charge of Jesus. Carrying his own cross, he went out to the place of the Skull (which in Aramaic is called Golgotha).

As they led him away, they seized Simon from Cyrene, who was on his way in from the country, and put the cross on him and made him carry it behind Jesus. A large number of people followed him, including women who mourned and wailed for him. Jesus turned and said to them, "Daughters of Jerusalem, do not weep for me . . ."

John 19:16-17, Luke 23:26-28

The Fifth Sorrowful Mystery

The Crucifixion

Here they crucified him. . . . Near the cross of Jesus stood his mother, his mother's sister, Mary the wife of Clopas, and Mary Magdalene. When Jesus saw his mother there, and the disciple whom he loved standing nearby, he said to his mother, "Dear woman, here is your son," and to the disciple, "Here is your mother." From that time on, this disciple took her into his home.

It was now about the sixth hour, and darkness came over the whole land until the ninth hour, for the sun stopped shining. And the curtain of the temple was torn in two. Jesus called out with a loud voice, "Father, into your hands I commit my spirit." When he had said this, he breathed his last.

John 19:18, 25-27, Luke 23:44-46

The Glorious Mysteries

The First Glorious Mystery

The Resurrection

The angel said to the women, "Do not be afraid, for I know that you are looking for Jesus, who was crucified. He is not here; he has risen, just as he said. Come and see the place where he lay. Then go quickly and tell his disciples: 'He has risen from the dead and is going ahead of you into Galilee. There you will see him.' Now I have told you."

So the women hurried away from the tomb, afraid yet filled with joy, and ran to tell his disciples. Suddenly Jesus met them. . . . "Do not be afraid. Go and tell my brothers to go to Galilee; there they will see me."

Matt. 28:5-10

The Second Glorious Mystery

The Ascension

So when they met together, they asked him, "Lord, are you at this time going to restore the kingdom to Israel?"

He said to them: "It is not for you to know the times or dates the Father has set by his own authority. But you will receive power when the Holy Spirit comes on you; and you will be my witnesses in Jerusalem, and in all Judea and Samaria, and to the ends of the earth."

After he said this, he was taken up before their very eyes, and a cloud hid him from their sight.

Acts 1:6-9

The Third Glorious Mystery
The Descent of the Holy Spirit

When the day of Pentecost came, they were all together in one place. Suddenly a sound like the blowing of a violent wind came from heaven and filled the whole house where they were sitting. They saw what seemed to be tongues of fire that separated and came to rest on each of them. All of them were filled with the Holy Spirit and began to speak in other tongues as the Spirit enabled them.

Acts 2:1-4

The Fourth Glorious Mystery

The Assumption of Mary

A great and wondrous sign appeared in heaven: a woman clothed with the sun, with the moon under her feet and a crown of twelve stars on her head.

Rev. 12:1

The Fifth Glorious Mystery

The Crowning of Mary

I delight greatly in the Lord; my soul rejoices in my God. For he has clothed me with garments of salvation and arrayed me in a robe of righteousness, as a bridegroom adorns his head like a priest, and as a bride adorns herself with her jewels.

Isa. 61:10

The Fourth Glorious Mystery
(Alternate)
The Second Coming

"When the Son of Man comes in his glory, and all the angels with him, he will sit on his throne in heavenly glory. All the nations will be gathered before him . . ."

Matt. 25:31-32

The Fifth Glorious Mystery
(Alternate)
The Kingdom of God

"I will give you the keys of the kingdom of heaven; whatever you bind on earth will be bound in heaven, and whatever you loose on earth will be loosed in heaven."

Matt. 16:19

Concluding Prayers

Hail, Holy Queen

Hail, holy Queen, Mother of Mercy! Our life, our sweetness, and our hope! To thee do we cry, poor banished children of Eve; to thee do we send up our sighs, mourning and weeping in this valley of tears. Turn, then, most gracious advocate, thine eyes of mercy toward us; and after this our exile show unto us the blessed fruit of thy womb Jesus; O clement, O loving, O sweet Virgin Mary.

Or

Jesus Prayer

Lord Jesus Christ, Son of the Living God, have mercy on me.

Sign of the Cross

In the name of the Father, and of the Son and of the Holy Spirit. Amen.

Art Credits

p. 28: Pietro Perugino, *Virgin and Child Between Saint Rose, Saint Catherine and Two Angels*, Louvre, Paris. Réunion des Musées Nationaux/Art Resource, NY.

p. 31: Sandro Botticelli, *The Annunciation*, Galleria degli Uffizi, Florence. Scala/Art Resource, NY.

p. 33: Domenico Ghirlandaio, *The Visitation* (detail), Louvre, Paris. Bridgeman Giraudon.

p. 35: Gentile da Fabriano, *Adoration of the Magi* (detail of *Mary with Child and King*), Galleria degli Uffizi, Florence. Erich Lessing/Art Resource, NY.

p. 37: Rembrandt van Rijn, *Presentation in the Temple*, National Museum, Stockholm. Kavaler/Art Resource, NY.

p. 39: Paris Bordone, *The Child Jesus Disputing in the Temple*, copyright © Isabella Stewart Gardner Museum, Boston. Bridgeman Art Library.

p. 40: James Jacques Joseph Tissot, *The Sermon on the Mount* (illustration for *The Life of Christ*), copyright © Brooklyn Museum of Art, New York. Bridgeman Art Library.

p. 43: Pietro Perugino, *The Baptism of Christ*, Kunsthistorisches Museum, Vienna. Erich Lessing/Art Resource, NY.

p. 45: Andrea Boscoli, *Wedding at Cana*, Galleria degli Uffizi, Florence. Bridgeman Art Library.

p. 47: Fra Angelico, *The Sermon on the Mount*, Museo de San Marco, Florence. Scala/Art Resource, NY.

p. 49: Raphael, *The Transfiguration* (detail), Pinacoteca, Vatican Museums, Vatican City. Scala/Art Resource, NY.

p. 51: Titian, *The Last Supper*, Galleria Nazionale delle Marche, Urbino, Italy. Scala/Art Resource, NY.

p. 52: Nikolai Ge, *Golgotha*, Tretyakov Gallery, Moscow. Scala/Art Resource, NY.

p. 55: Paul Gauguin, *The Agony in the Garden*, Norton Gallery, Palm Beach. Bridgeman Art Library.

p. 57: James Jacques Joseph Tissot, *The Scourging* (illustration for *The Life of Christ*), copyright © Brooklyn Museum of Art, New York. Bridgeman Art Library.

p. 59: Antonio Ciseri, *Ecce Homo*, Galleria d'Arte Moderna, Florence. Alinari/Art Resource, NY.

p. 61: Maurice Denis, *Calvary, or The Ascent to Calvary*, Musée d'Orsay, Paris. Réunion des Musées Nationaux/Art Resource, NY.

p. 63: El Greco, *Crucifixion*, Collection de la Mobilla, Seville, Spain. Scala/Art Resource, NY.

p. 64: Craigie Aitchison, *Landscape*, Private Collection. Bridgeman Art Library.

p. 67: Maurice Denis, *The Women Find Jesus' Tomb Empty (Luke 20:11-18)*, Musée du Prieuré, Saint-Germain-en-Laye, France. Erich Lessing/Art Resource, NY. Copyright © ARS, NY.

p. 69: Giotto di Bondone, *The Ascension of Christ*, Scrovegni Chapel, Padua, Italy. Cameraphoto/Art Resource, NY.

p. 71: Pieter Coecke van Aelst, *Pentecost*, Museo de Santa Cruz, Toledo, Spain. Bridgeman Art Library.

p. 73: Andrea del Sarto, The Poppi Altarpiece (*Assumption of the Virgin*), Galleria Palatina, Palazzo Pitti, Florence. Scala/Art Resource, NY.

p. 75: William-Adolphe Bouguereau, *The Virgin with Angels*, Musée du Petit Palais, Paris. Réunion des Musées Nationaux/Art Resource, NY.

p. 77: Enrico Scuri, *Let the Children Come Unto Me*, Private Collection, Milan. Scala/Art Resource, NY.

p. 79: *Last Judgment*, ceiling fresco in the sacristy of the abbey church of the Vorau, Abbey of the Augustinian Canons, Vorau, Austria. Erich Lessing/Art Resource, NY.

Acknowledgments

Thanks to my mentors Carole Baron, Victoria Skurnick, Sharon Fantera, Beth Goehring, Larry Shapiro, and Kathy Kiernan for their encouragement, humor, and insight. I hope I've made you all proud.

Thanks to Christos Peterson for designing this book and making a dream of mine come to life.

Thanks to Brad Miner, Andrea Doering, and Thomas Craughwell for your honesty, advice, and expertise.

Thanks to the following for their friendship (and for talking me down from the ledges of self-doubt): Audrey Puzzo, Deborah Sinclaire, Brigitte Weeks, Kalyani Fernando, Jay Franco, Lisa Thornbloom, John Webster, Loretta Holmes, Sandy Strk, Michelle Berger, Robin Posner, Lynette Daleo, Ericka Fergus, Cindy Karamitis, Jane Dentinger, Roger Cooper, Brian McCarthy, Lisa McCarthy, and Kimberly Cohen. You are all inspirations to me.

Thanks to Sam Honen, Joann Willig, Alaya Johnson, and my right-hand man, Justin Ravitz, for all your support and dedication.

Thanks to the four brothers I never had: Eric Hafker, Michael McCormack, William Romano, and Michael Stephenson. I'm blessed to know you and have you in my life.

Thanks to Father Andrzej Zglejszewski, Father Joseph Constantino, Lenny Tufaro, Al Prestinari, John Wright, Gerry Spagnolo, and all the retreatants at St. Ignatius Jesuit Retreat House.

Thanks to my father, lost, but not forgotten.

Thanks to my sisters Julie, Suzie, Mary, and Annie. You are all part of my heart.

Thanks to my Nana, Julia Powell, for always being one of my greatest cheerleaders. I'll always love you.

Thanks to Bert, Frances, Leonard, and Josephine Poppi for all the wonderful things you've done for me over the years.

Special thanks to my mom, Roseanne Jansen, for her courage and her faith. I love you deeply.

And lastly, thanks to my wife, Grace, and my son, Eddie, for blessing me with your love, faith, and wonder.